SHREE
GANESH

Written by

S. L. Goomar

Edited by

M. D. Gupta

Artwork by

Pritpal Singh

Published by

DREAMLAND PUBLICATIONS

Edition 1997

Printed at : Dewan Offset Printers (P) Ltd.

SHREE
卐 GANESH 卐

You must have read or seen, written or drawn 'Ganeshaya Namah' (Salutation to Ganesh) on the first page of a book or the front of houses, shops and in the opening of a ledger. It is also a common practice to worship Lord Ganesh by the side of goddess Lakshmi on the night of Diwali. Surely, you would like to know who Lord Ganesh or Ganeshji is and what place or importance He has in Hindu religion. He is called the god of wisdom. No auspicious act or ritual is begun without invoking Him.

It is a well-known fact that no action or effect takes place without a cause or reason. Now, the question rises why Ganesh had to take birth. For this purpose, we shall have to go through the pages of ancient history or mythology.

During the time between the end of Dwapar and the beginning of Kaliyug, performance of sacrifices or penance was neither austere nor rigid. Thus, mortal human beings started receiving the blessings of Lord Shiva by worshipping and pleasing Him in His shrine Someshwar or Somanath. By praying or worshipping Him simply, people could attain freedom from their sins. This meant salvation. Salvation was made easy for common men to get entry into the heaven.

The entrants to the heaven increased in great number. But they did not have the level of living and thinking as desired there. They indulged in wordly luxuries and were arrogant. They did not listen to the gods or the sages. Everyone thought, "I am the greatest. I am subordinate to none."

When the situation did not improve for a long time, the gods found themselves disturbed and perturbed. They were unable to perform any religious ritual or worship. It was impossible for them to find any clean and calm place to even live in. In other words, the heaven was no more the abode of gods as if inhabited by mortals. When the gods asked them to behave properly, they were insulted and abused. They pushed and elbowed the gods away. None could set them right. There was no peace in the heaven. There was everywhere mischief, disputation and breach of rules. Heaven had virtually become a hell. The gods were simply bewildered and dumb-founded at the odd behaviour of the mortals who were bent upon throwing out the gods from their ancient abode. The gods tried to intimidate the mortals by their impressive robes and looks but it proved to be an exercise in futility. Their angry looks merely emboldened the mortals. The gods were in a fix and did not know what to do.

3

At last, the gods presented themselves to Shiva for redressal of their problems.

The gods led by their King Indra, prayed to Shiva for His mercy and protection, "O Shankar ! It is not at all possible for us to live in the heaven. This place is overcrowded with large numbers of mortals. They include the learned as well as the ignorant. There are also good-doers and evil-doers too. They have neither control over themselves nor they care for any rules. They are impertinent and sinners too. This is the result of your blessings bestowed upon them and their number is increasing day by day. We find no suitable place for worship and no peace for this purpose. True, you are not bothered by anything but we fail to concentrate. We cannot attend to anything."

"After having failed in our efforts, we have come to pray to you to turn these lechers out of this godly place or keep them under your control. You should restrict their entry here. Please either save us from them who are worse than animals or direct us as to where we should go."

Lord Shiva listened very carefully to their tale of woes and said, "O Indra ! I cannot go against my own boon ! Go to Parvati she alone can solve your problem."

The gods had some solace in what Shiva had said. With great hope, they approached Parvati. They bowed to Her with great humility and prayed to Her, "O goddess ! we bow before you. You are the base of this Universe. We salute You again and again. We pray to You because You are the Creator and You are the Destroyer. Victory be to You ! O mother ! we seek your benediction. Please protect us. We have come to you. Who else can save us from this hour of distress ?"

Parvati looked at the pathetic and pitiable condition of Indra and gods. She took compassion on them. She said, "O Lord of gods ! you and your companion gods should be freed from this calamity. I feel so. Your demand will be fulfilled. Now, rest assured and go. Wait for some time, all will be well." Indra and other gods, once again requested the omniscient Parvati with folded hands that she alone could tackle their problems in a trice. They would be ever indebted to her as her grace was boundless. The Goddess Parvati raised her hand to bless the gods who bowed low out of deep reverence for her. Merrily and happily they took her leave.

Shiva had appointed some of his guards, who are called Ganas or soldiers outside the palace of Parvati. At the main gate of the inner palace, Shiva's troops were posted, whose chiefs were Nandi and Bhringi. As they were Shiva's Ganas, they considered themselves very important. There was none to question them and they themselves listened to none. On the other hand, the maidens in the palace had to obey the orders of Nandi and Bhringi. They were not free to go out of the palace or enter into it whenever they liked. These maidens did not like this system at all. Parvati came out of her palace and presented herself at the main gate. She was bare-footed. She must have been in a great hurry. It appeared from her looks that she was greatly perturbed and agitated. She beckoned Nandi with her right hand, the left resting on her girdle. She then invited Nandi's attention to pay heed to what she was going to say. Nandi at once stood to attention to listen to her. He seemed to be somewhat amazed. But nevertheless, he must listen to his mistress. Parvati commanded, "Nandi, you are in my service. You must not allow anyone to enter my palace without my prior permission ! But my dear friends Jaya and Vijaya are absolutely free to come in and go out at any moment and at all hours."

6

Parvati, being the mistress of the palace, had ordered her maidens not to let anybody enter her inner palace without her permission. Shiva never cared for any formalities. He used to go into even her personal rooms whenever he desired. Who could stop him ? Nandi and Bhringi had neither the courage nor the shrewdness to check Shiva. As soon as Shiva appeared at the gate of the palace to enter Parvati's apartment, Nandi stood dumb like a statue. He was reminded of Parvati's instructions but the overbearing personality of Lord Shiva held him in thraldom. He was very eager within his heart to stop Shiva from entering the palace but he dared not utter even a single word lest he should incur the wrath of Mahadeva. So Lord Shiva with great pride entered the palace much against the orders of Parvati which she had issued to Nandi. Now Nandi was shaken within his bosom. He was in deep distress. He did not know how to face Parvati. If she lost her temper, what curse of hers he would have to bear !

7

Parvati often felt offended and was at times even annoyed at the arrogance of the attendants who were not afraid of disobeying her orders. She considered it imprudent on the part of Nandi and Bhringi. There were many maidens in the service of Parvati. The main two of them were Jaya and Vijaya. They usually took liberty with her as they were very close to her. They considered themselves to be her privileged friends. They hated to talk to Nandi and Bhringi, not to speak of other attendants.

When Parvati saw Shiva in her palace all of a sudden without any information from Nandi and Bhringi, her surprise and anger knew no bounds. She was going to question Lord Shiva, but somehow or the other, she managed to restrain herself. She had lost the faith she had reposed in Nandi and Bhringi who had miserably failed in her eyes to guard her apartment according to her wishes and instructions. She had her own plans to guard herself.

Jaya and Vijaya used to speak ill of Nandi and Bhringi before Parvati within the premises of the palace. Whenever they had to speak to these attendants, they felt bad. Thus, both the maidens all the time pestered Parvati to do something to get rid of them.

Parvati was already greatly agitated in her mind regarding her security arrangements. She had seen how Shiva suddenly entered without her knowledge. She felt that she had no privacy at all. This was too much for her. Jaya and Vijaya seized this opportune moment to impress upon Parvati that she must go in for her own guard to make herself secure. They condemned Nandi and Bhringi with a free tongue. They must get due regards from the guards at the gate. But they were too rude to be tolerated. Parvati was deeply influenced by their heart to heart talks. She made up her mind to do something concrete in the matter so that Nandi and Bhringi's services could be terminated. She pondered deeply for a long time. All of a sudden an idea flashed through her mind, "Who could protect me better than my own son ?"

9

When the gods had approached Parvati for her favour, she decided to kill two birds with one stone. The other day, while taking her bath, she took some soil from the holy Ganges and a little of cosmetic material and made a figure of that clay.

She infused life into that figure. Then she dressed that boy like a prince and decorated him with ornaments and jewels. This figure was of Ganesha. Then she spoke to that boy in these words, "O Prince ! you are my son. You are entrusted with the job of guarding my personal apartment. You shall not permit anybody to enter this palace." As Ganesha had been created out of the clay and water of the Ganges, she said to Parvati, "O goddess ! I have also contributed towards the creation of this handsome boy. I too am his mother." This is why Ganesha is called "Dwimatri" (one who has two mothers).

The son who has two mothers must be exceptionally brave and brilliant. Bhishma in the Mahabharta's Shantiparva says that the mother is the greatest teacher and Guru. Her inportance is ten times greater than that of the father. Verily, Ganesha who enjoys the blessings of two mothers is the very embodiment of wisdom and valour. He is as pure and sacred as the Ganga herself who happens to be one of his mothers.

Ganesha bowed to Parvati and said with folded hands, "O mother ! I shall obey your orders. Don't worry." Saying so, he took a staff in one of his hands and stood guard at the door of the inner palace. Parvati was very happy. She left the place to take rest in her apartment. (In the meanwhile, Nandi and Bhringi saw that a young boy was standing outside the gate. Both of them were unable to find out who that young boy was. They also wondered what he was doing there. They questioned Ganesha who he was, but he did not reply. He, in fact, did not care to look at them. They were in a fix as to what they should do though they were greatly impressed by his looks.)

Who would not be impressed by Ganesha's looks ? Ganesha is the god of wisdom. He presides over our intellect. Man bereft of wisdom is worse than an animal. It is our common experience that a learned man exudes confidence. He can take others into confidence. He can cast a spell on others. So, Ganesha has been described as the 'Remover of all obstacles.' In fact, it is the wisdom that clears all hurdles in one's way.

11

After some time Lord Shiva came. Nandi and Bhringi showed their respects to him and told him about the presence of Ganesha inside the palace. He listened, but said nothing. He walked towards the gate of the personal apartment of Parvati. He saw Ganesh standing in front of the gate. He did not bother to look at or speak to Ganesha. When he did not stop at the gate, Ganesh tried to obstruct Shiva's way by placing himself in the middle of the door. Shiva stopped and thought, "Who is he to prevent me from getting in ?" He looked at the young man and said, "Who are you ?"

Ganesh, instead of replying to the question, asked Shiva, "Who are you ? My mother is taking her bath. You cannot enter this palace."

Shiva looked at him from head to foot and said, "I am the master of this palace. I am Shiva."

Ganesh got alert and said, "Shiva ! Who Shiva ? I don't know any such person. My duty is to guard this palace. I cannot let you step in."

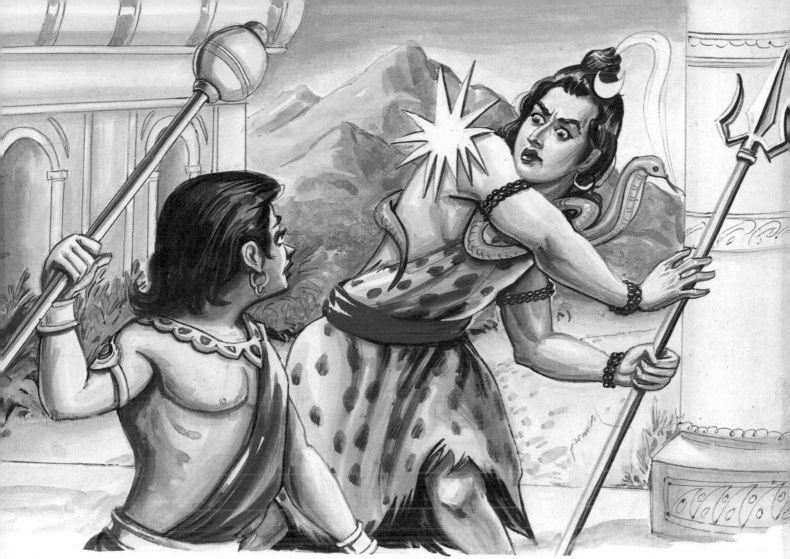

Shiva spoke, "Young man, get aside. This palace is mine and the mistress of the palace is also mine."

Saying this, Shiva stepped ahead in anger. Ganesh, without any hesitation, hit Shiva with his staff. Shiva turned and looked at him, but did nothing. He was shocked at the behaviour of Ganesh. He said to Nandi, "He is very insolent and rude. Push him out."

One is amazed and shocked to see Ganesha hitting Mahadeva with his staff. Moreover, Mahadeva feeling himself helpless could do nothing ! Why such a sorry state of affairs ! The reason is not far to seek. Shiva told Ganesha, "Get aside ! This palace is mine and the mistress of the palace is also mine." This attitude of possessiveness and arrogance would land anybody in trouble. Since nothing belongs to me how does my wife belong to me ? How does my palace or wealth belong to me ? He who commits this mistake of possessing wordly things must be hit with the staff of wisdom one day to rectify his mistake.

13

Nandi and his companions attacked Ganesh with the idea of punishing him. But, on the contrary, Ganesh thrashed them very hard. Shiva began feeling insulted. He did not deem it fit to punish the young boy himself. He was very angry. He left the place at once. Nandi and Bhringi had got their legs broken. They could not lay their hands on Ganesh. They were totally demoralised. When they all were helpless, they returned to Shiva's abode. They admitted their defeat and told him how brave and strong Ganesh was.

Shiva commanded his other Ganas and attendants, "Go and tell him he must behave properly. In case he does not understand, bring him here by force." Shiva's troops rushed towards Parvati's palace in great rage. Ganesh posted himself at the outer gate of the main palace lest they should force their entry into the inner palace. The troops first tried to make Ganesh see reason and understand who Shiva was. But Ganesh was not in a mood to listen to them. He repeatedly said, "My job is to guard the palace. This palace belongs to my mother. Without her permission, no body will be allowed to go inside. I have my duty to do. Now, you should go and do your duty."

Shiva's Ganas tried to intimidate Ganesha when he had asked them to go. Who could scare him ? When they threatened him of punishment, Ganesh lost his temper. He shouted, "Be off. Don't forget that I am Ganesh."

When Ganesh had flatly refused to listen to Shiva's troops, they charged at him. They thought that they would set him right.

14

A battle ensued between the army of Ganas on the one hand and Ganesh, the son of Parvati, alone on the other hand. The troops were armed with clubs, spears and axes. Their assault was immense. Ganesh wielded his mace and the enemy soldiers began to fall down injured and dead. There was a great commotion. They came to learn that the youngman was not an ordinary person. They were convinced that he did possess divine power. Perhaps the God of Death had come in disguise. Ganas were falling injured and dead, but Ganesh did not get even a bruise.

Shiva's troops, badly mauled and terrified, were disappointed and left Parvati's palace in a hurry. They were totally defeated. Nandi and Bhringi had been disgraced at Ganesha's hands. They never expected that he would punish them like a dog. Shiva was amazed at the plight of Nandi and Bhringi. On the other hand, disturbed at the turmoil, created by the battle between the Ganas of Shiva and Ganesh, the gods in the heaven and the sages on the earth, were alarmed and worried. They could not make out what was happening. They all reached the place of fight and at the site of the scene. They were shocked. Frightened of some imminent calamity, they approached Shiva and said, "Mahadeva ! What is all this?"

15

Shiva was already red hot with anger. He explained everything to them. He then said, "O Brahma ! you are the Creator. Will it not be desireable that you go and make him understand what is right and what is wrong. I wonder that there's none who can control this impertinent boy. Please go and see that he cools down. Otherwise, there may be devastation all around."

Brahma was silent. After contemplating over the matter for a few moments, he said, "Shankar ! you are losing your self-control. Everyone fears your anger."

Shiva controlled his anger somehow or the other. He said, "Brahma ! I want to tell you one thing quite plainly. And this is that this boy is not only foolish but also discourteous."

When Shiva had finished talking, Brahma said, "O Shiva ! please be calm and give up anger. We shall do what you wish."

Shiva replied, "You may go now. It is better that this ill-mannered boy is persuaded to behave as he should."

16

Brahma said, "You are right. I am going to him. I shall be in the guise of a mendicant. It may help him in cooling down and he may listen to a sage."

Brahma left Shiva's place, along with other gods in the guise of sages. This group of sages reached the outside of Parvati's palace where Ganesh was standing at guard. Brahma approached Ganesh with the idea of persuading him. On the other hand Ganesh thought they were the troops of Shiva in the guise of sages and had come to fight with him. Ganesh did not and could not recognise Brahma. He did not know that Brahma was one of the highest gods and commanded great respect. He did not know that he was the creator of this world in which he happened to dwell. Everybody bowed before Brahma. But Ganesha did not fear him at all. He did not recognise so many other great sages who had accompanied Brahma. Ganesha refused to listen to any one of them. He was bent upon doing his duty as a guard.

17

He raised his hand and caught hold of Brahma's beard in his fist. Brahma did not get the time even to speak a word to Ganesh. He was very much upset. However, he said, "No doubt, you are brave. But we are ascetics. We have not come to quarrel or fight with you as this is not our job. We are here to tell you that you should not cause flow of blood for nothing.

It is for the good of one and all. You don't know who we are and with whom you are fighting. You are not aware of your might and what power you possess."

Ganesh was agitated. He was not prepared to listen to any sermon from Brahma. He did not need advice of any kind. He was concerned with his duty only. Brahma's beard was in the grip of Ganesh and he pinched it. A bunch of hair from the beard was plucked in a jerk. Brahma could not say anymore. Brahma at once ran back. The other gods, who were in the guise, followed Brahma, leaving behind their begging bowls.

Brahma told everything to Shiva and Vishnu.

18

On the other hand, Parvati's maidens Jaya and Vijaya, came running to her and informed her that Ganesh was being assaulted by Shiva's Ganas. Shiva was fretting and fuming as Ganesh had offended him. She thought, "So, attempts are being made to kill my son. Shiva is my husband. Does it mean that I am of no importance ? I have no honour or respect of my own. Do I not have the right to have even my own security arrangements ? So, I shall not accept this situation. I shall not allow any person to interfere in any matter concerning me."

Manu, the Hindu Law Giver, in his famous work 'Manusmriti' has rightly pointed out, "Gods dwell where the women are respected and worshipped. But where they are not duly honoured, all the fruits and boons disappear." A husband must treat his wife on equal footing although she is superior to him in so many respects. An insulted and offended woman can cause great havoc as Parvati did. Let us seek some advice from this religious episode.

There was no end to Parvati's anger. She created two of her Shaktis (powers) Kali and Durga. These Shaktis presented themselves before Parvati and said, "O great goddess ! what are the orders for us ? We are ready to do anything you desire."

Parvati spoke in great fury, "O powerful ones ! Today, my son is in great distress. The irony is that Shiva himself is at the back of all this. He is bent upon humiliating and repressing him. At his command all the gods are attacking Ganesh while he is all alone. I want you to come forward to help and protect him. I cannot tolerate the very idea of his defeat or subjugation."

Shaktis replied, "It shall be so. We shall leave no stone unturned in fulfilling your wish. May we take your leave now." Taking orders from Parvati, they arrived at the place where Ganesh was standing to guard Parvati's palace.

20

Vishnu and Shiva were having deliberations. Visnhu said, "O Supreme one ! listen to my suggestion. The gods have failed to defeat Ganesh. We have only one option left with us and that is to kill this young boy by fair or foul means. Otherwise the heaven itself will become a battle field, without success in forcing him to surrender."

Shiva deliberated on Vishnu's proposal. The situation had become grave. He said, " I think you are right. I agree to your suggestion. Now, please go and see that this crisis is over for ever." Vishnu took Shiva's leave and reached where Ganesh was ready to face any one. Shiva was not confident of Vishnu's victory over Ganesh.

Why was Shiva not confident of Vishnu's victory over Ganesh ? The reason is so simple. Vishnu is the Preserver and Protector ! How can he go against his ownLaw ! He who preserves cannot kill. 'Vishnu' means that which is all-pervasive and omnipresent. It means he preserves every atom in the Universe. So the question of killing Ganesha does not arise at all. Shiva, who is the Destroyer, alone could have killed Ganesha.

Shiva followed Vishnu and other gods. The battle was in full fury. Vishnu, mounted on his vehicle Garud, was charging at Ganesh with his mace. The god's army was well-armed with all sorts of weapons including missiles. They attacked Ganesh. But, unfortunately for the gods, they faced the same fate as that of Ganas of Shiva. Goddess Kali was there to help Ganesh. She swallowed all the weapons hurled at him. As a result of this, he was unseathed. On the contrary, those arms turned back and destroyed Ganesh's enemies.

Durga, on her part, took the form of lightning. As soon as the arms of the god's soldiers touched the lightning, they were reduced to ashes. They did not get time even to reach Ganesha. When Lord Vishnu could not subjugate Ganesha inspite of his best efforts and techniques, he felt humiliated before a mere boy. He was red with rage. He picked up his sharp-toothed wheel—Sudarshan Chakra and hurled it at Ganesha's mace which was cut into two.

When Vishnu found that his planning had flopped, he readied himself to release his Sudarshan Chakra, the divine missile. Ganesh had only his mace or club with him. He tried to face the Shudarshan Chakra with it, but the divine missile could not be futile. So, Ganesh's mace bore the brunt of the missile and was broken into two. Ganesh was astonished and angry too. He hurled the broken piece of his mace at Vishnu's vehicle. Garuda grasped the handle of Ganesh's mace in his beak and thus saved Vishnu. Ganesh was then unarmed. He was agitated at the loss of his weapon. He was exposed to the attack and helpless.

Wise as he was, Ganesha ran to save his life. He had faced Vishnu boldly and fearlessly. He never lost his wits while fighting. He who is the lord of wits can never be deprived of his wisdom. Vishnu failed to Vanquish Ganesha inspite of all the resources at his disposal. Indeed, the greatest and the most effective weapon is wisdom itself which Ganesha did possess. This wisdom came to his rescue again and again.

At the same time, Shiva threw his Trishul. The Trishul was shot from the back side of Ganesh. The Trishul (Divine Trident) chopped off Ganesh's head. Vishnu was anxiously waiting for such a step to be taken. This was the wickedness of Vishnu which put an end to Ganesh's resistence towards Shiva and other gods. The gods heaved a sigh of relief that there would be no more army fighting. Shiva was also pacified.

But that was not so. When Parvati learnt of the news of his son's beheading, her shock and distress was endless. First she started wailing and crying, but then she composed herself. She got angry and her wrath knew no bounds. She said with determination, "If my son dies, I shall not let live anybody." All the gods and Dewas began to tremble when they heard Parvati's pronouncement. They were frightened of Parvati's anger.

24

The gods called Naradji. When Naradji came, they said, "O great sage ! you are omniscient and omnipresent. If any one can save this world from Parvati's fury, it is you. Therefore, we request you to go to her and try to pacify her." Naradji knew well that it was not possible. He was sure that Parvati would not listen to anybody. He was also not in a position to refuse to help the gods.

At Parvati's place he found that Parvati was burning red with rage. Narad was afraid of talking to her.

Parvati said, "Narad ! these gods have killed my son who was simply doing his duty. None of them took pity on a boy who had not done any harm. They call themselves just and brave. They have slain him mercilessly by adopting unfair means. This is their godliness and valour. I shall avenge his death. These gods will have to pay the price for this wild act of theirs. I am not going to spare these gods and the attendants of Shiva. I shall be the judge and all of them will be punished. Perhaps, they are not aware that they cannot escape the outcome of their misdeeds and the penalty thereof."

25

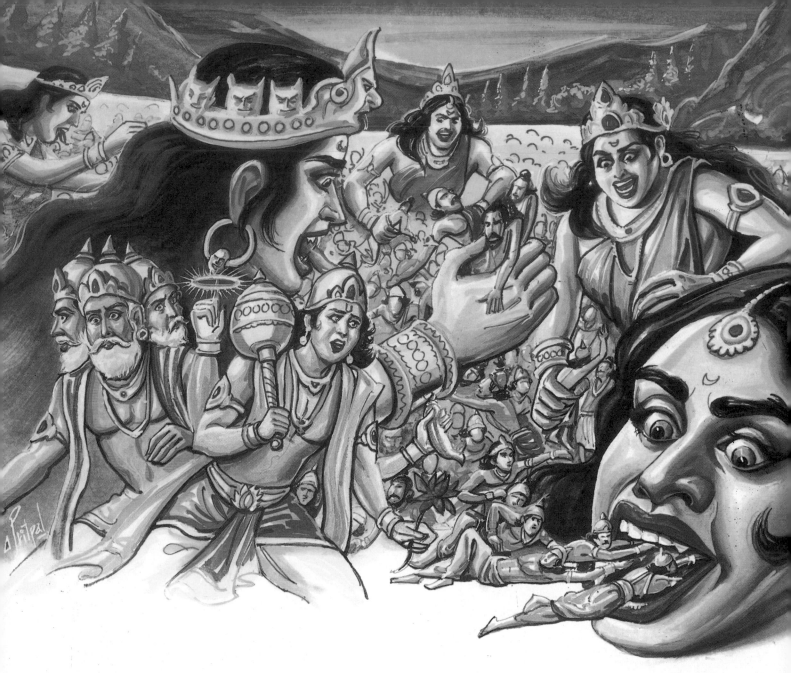

By that time, Parvati had lost control over her anger. She said to her Shaktis (power) and ordered, "Great wrong had been done to me. My son has been killed unjustly. I have to take revenge upon the gods and Shiva's Ganas. For this purpose, I seek your help. There is only one way for this. You shall punish them as should be done to the enemies and kill them all. They don't deserve any mercy."

Naradji was certain that no contrivance or sweet talk was going to help. He said, "O great goddess ! you are supreme. Your might is limitless. Similarly, you are large-hearted and benevolent. Out of your anger, you are being ruthless. This does not behove you. Please give up anger and calm down. You must punish the gods, but don't cause the whole universe to be devastated. This is not my advice, but my humble request to you. Have mercy and spare those who are not a party to the ghastly act."

26

Parvati was not affected as if she had not listened to what Naradji had said. She ordered her Shakti to go and do as asked. There was no sense in staying further with Parvati. He left the place and went straight to where Brahma and Vishnu were waiting for him.

Naradji explained the situation to them and warned them to what Parvati was going to do. On the other hand, Shakti's, commanded by Parvati, began beating, killing and devouring the gods and Shiva's troops wherever they chanced to come in their way.

Brahma and Vishnu did not have time to think. They rushed to Parvati to stop the carnage she had ordered.

When misfortune befalls a person, he loses his capacity to think. Even Brahma and Vishnu failed to think a way out when Parvati's Shaktis caused widespread destruction of the gods and their troops. It was the case of the wrath of a woman ?

27

Brahma and Vishnu went to Parvati with great fear in their minds as they were afraid of her wrath. They prayed to her, "O exalted one ! Have pity on us. Only God knows how we lost our senses. We had not realised how great and brave your son was. Having been frightened by him, we have committed this sin. We solicit your forgiveness. We submit to you and are ready to accept any punishment you deem fit. We have come here to do whatever you order us to do. Please stop this catastrophy."

The pleadings and prayers of Brahma and Vishnu pacified Parvati to some extent. She said, "O Creator of the Universe ! Do you both think that what has been done is forgiveable or forgettable ? Can a mother condone the murder of her son ? Never ! I can pardon you, but on my condition."

Brahma said, "Please do tell what you desire. We are willing to accept any condition you impose."

Parvati said, "Then, listen, Brahma ! you are the Creator. You have to grant life to my Ganesh. He shall be worshipped also a god as well."

Brahma said, "I agree to do so."

28

Brahma and Vishnu were so scared that they could not utter a sound. They did not expect Parvati in such a furious state of mind. They found themselves helpless. From there, they went to Shiva and informed him of all that had been said by Parvati. They also told him of the condition Parvati had put before them. They said, "O Shankar ! There is no time to waste. It is not possible for us to restrain the forces let loose by Parvati. Therefore, we should agree to her demands and save this Universe. Please go yourself and pacify her. How long shall you avoid her ? O Lord ! Be quick lest everything should be ruined or doomed."

Shiva could do nothing except agreeing to what Brahma had suggested. But, it was also not easy to face Parvati at the moment. He was thinking, "What will happen now ? No doubt, I have been reckless and done injustice to Parvati. She has lost her son. Being Parvati's son, Ganesh is my son too. What should I do ? The only alternative appears to be seeking her pardon. She has to be pacified at any cost. Shiva was feeling repentant for having killed Ganesha in a fit of rage. Now he was calm and composed. He was thinking deeply how he could pacify Parvati, his consort.

Shiva raised his head and said, "Well whatever Parvati says or sets any condition of her choice is acceptable to us. Of course we have committed a crime. We have to undo or counter what we have done. Parvati must be relieved of her overwhelming grief as justice must prevail. Certainly there is no other way out. Only a mother knows how she feels the shock of her affliction. There is no use of discussion or argumentation. So, O Brahma ! Chop off the head of the living being you see first in the morning in the direction of the north. Then bring that severed head to me. After replacing that head on the torso of this young boy, you may please infuse life into the body. Parvati will get her son. This is how we can appease her. After that I shall visit her and the imminent destruction shall be warded off. If you are prepared to do so, Parvati can be pacified."

Brahma and Vishnu took off and Shiva began to wait for the next morning. Brahma did as advised by Shiva. Next morning, he sent the gods to the forest in search of some living being. At the break of dawn, they saw an elephant. They cut off its head and brought that to where the torso of Ganesh was lying on the ground.

30

After having placed and joined the head and the torso of Ganesh, Brahma infused life into that. Ganesh came to life and got up. Brahma took Ganesh, with elephant's head, to Parvati's palace. Vishnu was also with him. On their way, he said to Brahma, "Has it come to your mind or not how Parvati would react to this act of yours when she sees Ganesh with an elephant's head ? What shall you do if she does not approve of it ?"

Brahma was shocked at what Vishnu had said. He had really not thought over that. He agreed with Vishnu that they had taken a hasty step. He was non-plussed and could not take a step further. He pondered for some time. Then he said, "Vishnu ! It is true that we have not given any thought to the pros and cons of what we have done. We have simply followed the advice of Shiva. We have brought life to Parvati's son in good faith. No blame should be put on us ? Moreover, I don't distinguish between a god and a man or an animal. So, far as I am concerned, all are equal. They are all living beings."

Vishnu said, "Let us go. Let us presume that Shankar has given due consideration to everything. We all are bound by destiny."

31

Vishnu followed Brahma who was leading Ganesh to Parvati. When she saw her son alive, her joy knew no bounds. She made him sit by her side with great affection and kissed him on his head. But she had not forgotten the other condition. However, the crisis was over. Parvati said to Brahma, "I am happy that I have my son back but what about his elevation to godhood ? You are silent about his status."

Brahma and Vishnu had not discussed this issue with Shiva. In fact, they had forgotten it. Brahma was speechless. He was scared and so was Vishnu.

Brahma could think of no excuse. There was no reply to the question raised by Parvati. He was in no position to say yes or no as nothing was in his or Vishnu's hand. So, they started saying, "O great mother of Ganesh ! We........"

Shiva appeared there before Brahma could explain what he had in mind. Shiva looked at Parvati to find out whether she was still furious or was pacified and pleased to get Ganesh back alive.

Parvati was very happy to see her husband. He said, "I am guilty of yours and beg your pardon. The condition put by you is acceptable to us. I give the promise, in the presence of these gods, that Ganesh will be recognised my son. He will be the chief of my Ganas. He will be called "Ganapati". All of my troops and attendants will obey his orders. What else do you want ?"

Parvati kept quiet for some time. Then she said, "Mahadeva ! I wish my son to be invincible and giver of victory to whom he likes to give. He who worships him, should obtain success and prosperity. Ganesh be the giver of wisdom. Whenever and wherever any god is worshipped and offered oblations, Ganesh will be first to be adorned and appeased. No body should be permitted to the heaven before pleasing him. O Shiva ! you accept him as your son.

You shall make it compulsory for one and all to take Ganesh's permission for admission before you. Moreover, whenever invoked, Ganesh should have the power to remove the obstacles in the way of his devotees. O Lord ! I pray to you to favour him with your blessings. This is my desire." "Be it so !" said Shiva.

Parvati had cooled down. As asked by Shiva, she smiled and looked at the gods benevolently. The fire of her anger had subsided. She had won and the gods had been vanquished. She looked into the sky, signalled to her Shaktis and soon there was tranquility and happiness all over. Brahma and Vishnu, along with other gods, rejoiced. They bowed before Parvati and Shiva. After blessing Ganesh, they took their leave.

Shiva was glad that he had been able to correct his mistake. Parvati was delighted that the gods had been taught a good lesson that none can save them from their evil or wrong deeds. Above all, her son had attained godhood.

After normalcy had prevailed in the heaven, Ganesh took charge of guarding the place of Shiva. Ganesh was the master there. There was none to bully or threaten him. Who could suppress or obstruct him ? He himself was the remover of all hindrances or obstacles in the way of others.

34

Once, Parshuram came to meet Shiva. Parshuram was a great devotee of Shiva and was also very proud of the fact that he was free to approach Shiva at any time he wished. When he reached the gate of Shiva's abode, he was stopped by Ganesh as he used to check everybody there. He had made it a rule. Ganesh said, "You cannot enter inside at this moment."

Parshuram said, "Why ?"

Ganesh said, "Mahadeva is having a nap. Nobody can disturb him while he is taking rest."

Parshuram, being very short-tempered by nature and always ready to quarrel, said, "Get aside. I am Parshuram. I have to see him immediately. I have no time to wait."

Ganesha said, "If you have no time to wait, I shall make you wait as I wait for persons like you at this gate !" Then Ganesha lifted Parshuram in his arms.

35

Ganesh was not impressed and did not budge an inch. He said, "O respected saint ! calm down. It is not possible. Come some other time." Parshuram had no patience. He got ready to fight with Ganesh. They came to blows. Ganesh entangled Parshuram in his trunk and twisted him around. Parshuram started feeling giddy and ultimately was unconscious.

Ganesh put Parshuram on the ground. When Parshuram came out of swoon, he found himself lying on the ground. He was furious. He was not in the habit of putting up with an insult. How could he tolerate that humiliation. He raised his battle-axe and threw it towards Ganesh. When Ganesh saw that weapon, he was immobile. He was helpless. He could not catch hold of or throw that away because that axe had been gifted as a present to Parshuram by Shiva when he had worshipped and pleased him. Ganesh recognised the axe.

What could Ganesh do ? He could not make Shiva's battle-axe ineffective. Assault by that divine weapon meant sure death. Ganesh took the axe by one of his tusks. As its result, that tusk was broken and Ganesh was left with one tusk only Because of this he is also called "Ekadanta" (one who has one tooth).

36

You must have read in the "Mahabharata" that it was Ganesh who had written this work. When sage Vedavyasa thought of writing "Mahabharat", he came to the conclusion that it would not be possible for him to pen down such a great volume by himself. He needed some well-read person who could follow and write what the sage would speak. He did not find a scholar who would help him, amongst the gods or mortals. Everyone avoided that stupendous job.

When Vedavyasa could not solve the problem, he went to Brahma and said, "O Lord ! I have decided to compose "Mahabharat". But the problem is that it is not possible for me to think, express and write such a huge volume alone. I need assistance of such a person who can note down correctly what I say. It is essential that every verse, I speak, must be understood well before being penned down."

Brahma said, "O honourable sage ! this idea of yours is excellent and I appreciate it very much. You deserve gratitude of all. Such a work, you desire to get done,

can be very safely entrusted to Ganesh. He is surely competent to do justice to this job. If you can appease and bring Ganesh round, your desire will be fulfilled."

Vedavyasa went to Ganesh and requested him, "O Lord of Shiva's Ganas ! You are the giver of wisdom and success. I stand in need of your help."

Ganesh said, "I shall do as you wish. But you shall meet one demand of mine."

"What is that ?" Vedavyasa said.

Ganesh replied, "You shall go on speaking and I shall go on writing. You should keep in mind that if you stop to speak, my concentration will be disturbed by other thoughts. If I lose concentration, you shall not blame me for any laxity in my work."

Vedavyasa was surprised. He said, "I have not followed what you mean to say."

Ganesh said, "The fact is that I cannot sit idle. I shall not waste time. If you are confident that you can do so, I am willing to assist you."

Vedavyasa understood what Ganesh meant. He smiled in his heart and said, "O remover of all obstacles ! I am ready to accept your demand. But I think you too well know that you shall not proceed to scribe before following the meaning of any verse. This is actually very essential to understand every verse before putting it to pen. I hope you agree with me that it is neither possible nor desirable to write a thing without understanding it. Ganesh agreed. Vedavyasa began to speak and Ganesh began to write. After dictating eulogical verses, Vedavyasa started telling the story. Whenever Vedavyasa stopped finishing a sentence, Ganesh at once said, "You are lagging behind. Increase your speed. Stopping makes me restless."

Vedavyasa increased his speed. Ganesh wrote faster. In short there was a competition between the two. Vedavyasa found that Ganesh could write faster than he could speak. In the end, his verses became more difficult and complex. Consequently, Ganesh had to take more time to grasp the purport of what Vedvyasa spoke. This gave time to him to think before dictating a verse.

Ganesh knew what Vedvyasa was doing and he could not compete with him. Then both of them gave up the race and became normal and stopped pulling each other's leg. Thus "Mahabharat" was completed smoothly and to the satisfaction of Vedavyasa.

The name of Ganesh's brother was karthikeya. When they had grown up, they said to their parents, "We have crossed the age of celibacy and should enter wedlock. For this we seek your permission to get married."

Shiva and Parvati were glad to hear this news. But then a question arose in their mind, "Who should be married first ?" They did not like to annoy either. Therefore, they said, "We welcome your idea. You both should go around the world and he who returns first will get married first."

Karthikeya took off immediately, but Ganesh did not like the idea of undertaking such an arduous and long journey. He made his parents sit at a place and circumnavigated seven times around them. Then said, "Look ! I have gone around the world not once but seven times."

Shiva said, "How it can be ?"

Ganesh said, "It is said in the Vedas that circumnavigation of parents is as sacred as going around the world."

Shiva and Parvati had no answer. Ganesh was married. When Karthikeya returned and learnt of Ganesh's trick, he was shocked and agitated. He vowed not to marry at all.

Due to this, he is called "Kumar" (one who remains unmarried).